Strategic Studies Institute
and
U.S. Army War College Press

ISLAMISM AND SECURITY
IN BOSNIA-HERZEGOVINA

Leslie S. Lebl

May 2014

*****

Comments pertaining to this report are invited and should be forwarded to: Director, Strategic Studies Institute and U.S. Army War College Press, U.S. Army War College, 47 Ashburn Drive, Carlisle, PA 17013-5010.

*****

*****

The Strategic Studies Institute and U.S. Army War College Press publishes a monthly email newsletter to update the national security community on the research of our analysts, recent and forthcoming publications, and upcoming conferences sponsored by the Institute. Each newsletter also provides a strategic commentary by one of our research analysts. If you are interested in receiving this newsletter, please subscribe on the SSI website at *www.StrategicStudiesInstitute.army.mil/newsletter.*

FOREWORD

Many observers viewed the military mission of the North Atlantic Treaty Organization (NATO) mission to Bosnia-Herzegovina (Bosnia), launched in late-1995, as a test of the international community's ability to keep the peace in the post-Cold War world. This task proved difficult: The many obstacles to restoring stability and growth in Bosnia have been thoroughly dissected over the years, from the challenges of transition governments to the difficulties of interethnic reconciliation.

One factor, however, has received but scant attention: the role of Islamism, the political ideology based on a religion that motivates the Muslim Brotherhood, al-Qaeda, and many other radical groups. This monograph will examine the impact of Islamism on Bosnian security, tracing developments during the 9 years of NATO peacekeeping, as well as the ensuing years. It will also examine the ties between so-called "nonviolent" and "violent" Islamism—ties that have already surfaced in other countries where NATO or the U.S. military is engaged. As a consequence, the monograph offers a framework to analyze the potential constraints that Islamism can place on present-day and future military missions in Muslim countries.

Douglas C. Lovelace

DOUGLAS C. LOVELACE, JR.
Director
Strategic Studies Institute and
U.S. Army War College Press

ABOUT THE AUTHOR

LESLIE S. LEBL is a Fellow of the American Center for Democracy and a Principal of Lebl Associates. A former Foreign Service Officer, she now writes, lectures, and consults on political and security matters. During her Foreign Service career, Ms. Lebl served as Political Advisor to the Commander of Stabilization Forces (SFOR) in Bosnia-Herzegovina in the late-1990s, first in the American sector in Tuzla and then at SFOR headquarters in Sarajevo. Her most recent publications include articles in *Orbis* on the European Union, the Muslim Brotherhood, and the Organization of Islamic Cooperation, and on radical Islam in Europe. A monograph, *Advancing U.S. Interests with the European Union*, was published by the Atlantic Council of the United States. Other publications include analyses of European defense policy for the Cato Institute and of U.S.-EU cooperation in combating terrorism for *Policy Review*. Ms. Lebl holds a B.A. in history from Swarthmore College and an M.A. in foreign affairs from the Johns Hopkins School of Advanced International Studies.

SUMMARY

Bosnia-Herzegovina, once thought to be on the way to joining the North Atlantic Treaty Organization (NATO) and the European Union (EU), is instead falling behind, mired in political bickering, economic stalemate, and governmental dysfunction. In this difficult situation, Islamism poses a significant threat to Bosnia's fragile domestic stability. Although the levels of Islamist terrorism and separatist movements are comparable to those elsewhere in Europe, they are particularly troublesome in Bosnia for two reasons. First, senior political and religious Bosniak (Muslim) leaders have long-standing ties to the Muslim Brotherhood and Islamist terrorism, including al-Qaeda and Iran, that they are very reluctant to abandon. Second, Islamism contributes significantly to Bosnia's dysfunction as a country. Calls to re-impose traditional Islamic law, or *sharia*, arouse opposition from Bosnian Serbs and Croats, as does the nostalgia for the Ottoman Empire and Islamic Caliphate shared by key Bosniak leaders, the Organization of Islamic Cooperation (OIC), and the Turkish government.

Some analysts think that Bosnia's slide can be reversed by mounting another NATO military mission, while others want the United States to accelerate its NATO membership. The U.S. Army should be prepared to explain why the previous NATO mission was successful, and why, in contrast, another one would be much more difficult. The European Command and the Office of the Secretary of Defense should alert Washington policymakers to the danger to NATO policymaking and day-to-day operations arising from the Islamist ties of some Bosniak leaders and representatives.

ISLAMISM AND SECURITY
IN BOSNIA-HERZEGOVINA

BOSNIA IN TROUBLE

Eighteen years after the fighting ended in Bosnia-Herzegovina (Bosnia), its territorial integrity and internal stability are not yet assured. Most observers had assumed that membership in the North Atlantic Treaty Organization (NATO) and the European Union (EU) would cement Bosnian security. Although other Balkan countries have successfully joined those two organizations,[1] Bosnia is unlikely to follow them any time soon. Instead, reforms that appeared to pave the way for membership have stalled. The unity of the state is in doubt; its governmental structure is unworkable, and its economy is failing.

The Bosnian governmental structure set up under the Dayton Peace Accords included a weak central state, two entities (the Bosniak-Croat Federation and the Serb Republic), and a separate jurisdiction for the disputed town of Brčko. With the Federation further divided into 10 relatively autonomous cantons—roughly reflecting the territorial divisions between Bosniaks and Croats—not only is the result top-heavy and unwieldy, but the structure encourages disputes and tensions framed in terms of ethnicity. Most observers, with the exception of the U.S. Government, have concluded that the cumbersome mechanism of two entities and a weak central state agreed to at Dayton in 1995 simply does not work.[2]

If Bosnia's economy were thriving, these tensions would probably recede. But basic requirements for such a thriving economy, such as large-scale energy projects, are frequently blocked by the lack of inter-

1

entity cooperation.[3] In addition, the economic liberalization required for growth would deprive the multiple layers of officialdom of substantial income, whether from controlling state-owned companies inherited from the communist past or revenues from the welter of existing regulations and administrative requirements.

Strong leadership might overcome this inertia, but strong leadership is exactly what is lacking. Meanwhile, corruption remains widespread,[4] and the average Bosnian faces high unemployment, reaching 57 percent among young people.[5] Poverty is mitigated by extensive state subsidies that further weigh down the economy and by black market jobs.

Former Serbian president Slobodan Milošević and former Croatian president Franjo Tudjman famously divided up Bosnia on a napkin in 1991.[6] They failed to achieve their goal during the subsequent war, but the division of Bosnia from within has advanced apace. The poor economy has contributed to this process, but so has the deliberate policy of alienation pursued by all three ethnic groups. An entire generation of Bosnians has gone through an ethnically segregated educational system in which each group is taught its own version of religion, geography, history, and language.[7] Those divisions are then perpetuated by politicians who exploit ethnic fears and tensions.

Unsurprisingly, the inter-ethnic reconciliation hoped for at Dayton has not come to pass. Rather, an overwhelming majority of Bosnian Serbs support the secession of the Serb Republic. A large number of Croats have already left the country; they are estimated now to account for only 10 percent of Bosnia's population, as compared with 17 percent in 1991.[8] Of those Croats still in country, over 40 percent want to carve a third, Croat, entity out of the Federation,[9] despite the fact that the Dayton quota system currently grants them outsize influence (one-third of the state-level positions and half of those in the Federation government).

As Bosnian analysts Anes Alic and Vildana Skocajic put it, the majority of Bosnians "do not feel that this is their 'homeland'."[10] This puts an alarming spin on other, already-disturbing data: some 87 percent feel the country is going in the wrong direction,[11] and 77 percent of young people say they would leave Bosnia if they could.[12] Such negative perceptions are also typical of a country in demographic decline, as Bosnia is today.[13] It may be only mid-ranked on the list of failed states, but it is clearly in trouble.[14]

Neither NATO nor the EU can solve these problems, despite their best efforts. NATO provided first the Implementation Force (IFOR) and then its successor, Stabilization Force (SFOR), to maintain stability for 9 years after the war. Today, it maintains a military headquarters in Sarajevo to assist Bosnia with reforms and commitments related to NATO accession.

Bosnia has met all NATO membership requirements except for the registration of all the defense facilities deemed necessary for future defense as properties of the central state.[15] The Serb Republic has refused to transfer its properties, and its President, Milorad Dodik, has called for Bosnia to demilitarize rather than join NATO.[16] Clearly, the obstacles to NATO accession are political and can be removed only by the Bosnians themselves. Even if they are overcome, NATO has no means to solve Bosnia's serious social and economic problems.

EU accession, which requires extensive economic, social, and political reforms, is often viewed by U.S.

policymakers as the critical means to achieve Euro-Atlantic integration. One could argue that the EU is an unlikely tool for streamlining governments and reducing the public sector, promoting entrepreneurship rather than redistribution, and resolving cultural tensions among different groups. Nevertheless, the EU has prodded Bosnia, *inter alia*, to strengthen its central state institutions, reform its public administration and judicial system, combat corruption, and develop a market economy, but with only limited success. Today, EU officials appear to have concluded that there is not much they can do to solve Bosnia's problems, given Bosnian politicians' lack of vision and internecine disputes.[17] The EU official in charge of accession has warned that, if the present situation persists, Bosnia's application could be "frozen."[18]

If Bosnia was a just another EU candidate country, such an assessment would probably attract little attention. But in this case, it is significant, given the huge EU effort to rebuild Bosnia. The EU replaced SFOR with its own military operation, European Union Force (EUFOR); it replaced the United Nations (UN) police mission with the European Union Police Mission, and for a time it combined the position of EU Special Representative in Bosnia and Herzegovina with that of the UN's Office of the High Representative (OHR). in an effort to coordinate and direct the civilian international community's involvement in Bosnia. The failure of such an ambitious effort explains why Europeans now say that it is primarily up to the Bosnians, not outsiders, to fix Bosnia's problems.[19]

ISLAMISM: MUSLIM BROTHERS, TERRORISTS, AND WAHHABIS

In this precarious environment, the growth of Islamism is particularly worrisome. Islamism contrasts strongly with the more-moderate form of Islam traditionally practiced in Bosnia. A 20th century political ideology based on a religion, Islamism's ultimate goal is to replace Western law with traditional Islamic law, or *sharia*, worldwide. Not only would this undermine Western democracy by rejecting the laws designed by democratically elected representatives, but *sharia*'s fundamental principles — such as inequality before the law (more on this topic later in the text) — are antithetical to Western law. This transformation to Islamism would be accomplished by means of a global Caliphate, or Islamic empire, headed by a person who is both a political and religious leader.

Most Western observers dismiss warnings about the dangers of Islamism as crude Serb or Croat propaganda intended to undermine the Bosnian state. In so doing, they usually note that Islamism is unlikely to become a significant force because most Bosniaks continue to adhere to their traditionally moderate and relatively secular version of Islam. However, evidence drawn primarily from Bosniak and Western sources reveals a more-nuanced and alarming picture. To understand this picture, it is first necessary to identify the main types of Islamism influencing Bosnia today.

Islamists are usually divided into two categories: the violent Islamist who pursues holy war, or *jihad*, openly, and his nonviolent counterpart who publicly eschews it — except against Israel or Western forces fighting in Muslim countries. However, the links between violent and nonviolent Islamism, while often denied, are increasingly obvious. This is particularly true in countries like Egypt, Libya, Tunisia, and Syria, where the Muslim Brotherhood—the best-known group in the nonviolent category—now contends openly for power. The evidence from Bosnia presented later in this text also shows a blurred line between violence and nonviolence.

Instead, it is more useful to distinguish among three main groups of Islamists in Bosnia: those linked to the Muslim Brotherhood, a group whose members participate in democratic institutions and often publicly espouse Western values; those engaged in terrorist activity, or *jihad*; and so-called Wahhabis, adherents of Saudi fundamentalism who reject Western institutions. Some Wahhabis are linked to terrorist activity, while others are not. There are tensions and disputes among the three groups, but they all agree on the goal of replacing Western law with *sharia*. And all three groups have connections to the Bosniak political and religious elite.

The Muslim Brotherhood.

Islamism first appeared in Bosnia in 1941 when Alija Izetbegović and others formed the Young Muslims, a group patterned after the Muslim Brotherhood. Izetbegović's famous political tract from the early-1970s, the *Islamic Declaration*, contained many Islamist concepts, confirming his personal attraction to the ideology.

This ancient history suddenly sprang to life when Izetbegović founded a political party with former Young Muslims as its inner core, outmaneuvered his more-moderate rivals, and became president of Bosnia in 1990. He filled that position during and after the

Bosnian war, from 1990-96, and then became a member of the joint presidency (which rotates between a Serb, a Croat, and a Bosniak) from 1996-2000. He died in 2003, but his legacy lives on, as his long-time associate, Haris Silajdzić, and son, Bakir, follow in his footsteps, both as presidents of Bosnia and as Islamist sympathizers.

Brotherhood ties today are very important to another senior Bosniak, Mustafa Cerić. Cerić served for years as Grand Mufti of Sarajevo and the head of the official Islamic Community. In addition, he is considered to be a leading Bosniak political figure in his own right.

Thus, while little is said or written about Muslim Brotherhood activities in Bosnia, the most senior Bosniak leaders—viewed by Westerners as representing moderate, relatively secular Muslims—are, in fact, closely connected to, or deeply sympathetic with, that organization. Their views and their relationships steer Bosnia toward Islamism and the Muslim world, while alienating Bosniaks from Bosnian Serbs and Croats, their fellow citizens.

Terrorists.

Islamism received a tremendous boost with the arrival of Islamic fighters, or *mujahideen*, to fight on the Bosniak side during the 1992-95 war. Their military value has been disputed, but the accompanying financial and military support from Saudi Arabia and Iran was vital to the Bosniak war effort. While those two countries are rivals, they arrived at an accommodation in Bosnia to support the *mujahideen*. Saudi Arabia focused on financing and logistical supplies, and Iran on importing the fighters and on military aid.[20]

The war in Bosnia definitely gave al-Qaeda a huge boost, both in terms of organization and recruitment,[21] and helped radicalize European Muslims. Many of them were revolted by graphic videos of suffering Bosniaks, and some traveled to Bosnia to provide aid or fight and so came into contact with foreign *jihadists*. Many *jihadists* later directed their fighting skills against European and American targets. Since the war ended in 1995, Bosnian veterans from various countries have figured in terrorist activities in countries around the globe, among them France, Indonesia, Iraq, Malaysia, Morocco, Russia, Saudi Arabia, Spain, Thailand, the United Kingdom, the United States, and Yemen.[22]

The best-known initiatives to combat Islamist terrorism were the 1996 IFOR raid on an Iranian-run terrorist training camp in Pogorelica and numerous steps taken after the terrorist attacks of September 11, 2001 (9/11), on the United States. At that time, SFOR interrupted terrorist plots aimed at NATO and other Western targets and raided the Saudi High Commission and other Saudi charities that were funding terrorist organizations.

By 2004, terrorism expert Evan Kohlmann, in a book warning about the Afghan-Bosnian terrorist connection, concluded that al-Qaeda had largely failed to take root in Bosnia. He noted the progress made in shutting down various terrorist operations and expressed the opinion that al-Qaeda had failed because moderate Bosniaks rejected its extremist ideology.[23] However, Kohlmann may have spoken too soon. Box 1 shows a continuum from 1996 through 2006 in which Bosnia served as an active link in the al-Qaeda network.

Box 1

The "Bosnian Connection" in International Islamist Terror.

- Starting in 1996, senior *mujahideen* leaders such as Abu el-Ma'ali and Abu Sulaimann al-Makki, then living as "civilians" in Bocinja Donja, oversaw plots in France, Italy, and Jordan designed to avenge the deaths of other leaders.
- In 2008, the Office of the High Representative (OHR) in Sarajevo reportedly uncovered evidence that senior Bosniak politician Hasan Čengić signed off on a money transfer intended to finance the attacks of 9/11.
- Karim Said Atmani, the document forger for the group plotting the 2000 Millenium plot bombing, was a frequent visitor to Bosnia. He obtained his first Bosnian passport in 1995 and subsequently was allowed to stay without a valid passport after he was deported by Canada in 1998.
- In late-October 2001, Algerians with Bosnian citizenship were arrested by the Bosnian authorities on charges of plotting to fly small aircraft from Visoko and crash them into SFOR bases in Tuzla and Bratunac.
- The 2005 plot to bomb the funeral of Pope John Paul II in Croatia reportedly originated in Gornja Maoča. The plot involved smuggling rocket launchers, explosives, and detonators into Italy.

- Also in 2005, Bosnian police raided an apartment connected to a group seeking to blow up the British Embassy in Sarajevo, seizing explosives, rifles, other arms, and a video pledging vengeance for *jihadists* killed in Afghanistan and Iraq. One of those arrested, a Swedish citizen of Bosnian origin, ran a website on behalf of Abu Musab Zarqawi, head of al-Qaeda in Iraq.
- In 2006, a group of Bosnians and Macedonians linked to al-Qaeda were arrested in northern Italy after smuggling some 1,800 guns into that country from Istanbul.

Sources: Evan F. Kohlmann, *Al-Qaida's Jihad in Europe: The Afghan-Bosnian Network*, New York, Berg, 2004, pp. 176, 199, 201-209; *Bosnia-Herzegovina Federation public TV*, May 5, 2008; *The Washington Post*, March 11, 2000; *Channel 4 News*, January 17, 2002; *ISN*, November 17, 2008; *The Washington Post*, December 1, 2005; and Christopher Deliso, *The Coming Balkan Caliphate: The Threat of Radical Islam to Europe and the West*, Westport, CT: Praeger, 2007, p. 26.

Nor were the Iranians routed after the 1996 raid in Pogorelica. Today, both the Iranian Ministry of Intelligence and National Security (VEVAK) and the Islamic Revolutionary Guards Corps (IRGC) have a presence in Bosnia. Of the two, the IRGC reportedly has the better, more-extensive network.[24] After the July 2012 terrorist attack at the Burgas airport in Bulgaria, international attention focused on possible threats from Hezbollah elsewhere in the Balkans. An Israeli expert, cited by Christopher Deliso, concluded that Bosnia posed the biggest danger in the region because "There remain pro-Iranian elements in the government, and

Iran is active through the embassy in Sarajevo and charities."[25]

Today, Islamist terrorism persists in Bosnia, whether involving al-Qaeda, Iran, or home-grown sources, but assessments of the threat it poses vary. Many Western analysts largely have dismissed this terrorism as not being a major issue. The 2013 Congressional Research Service report on Bosnia, for example, makes only a brief mention of terrorism,[26] and recent State Department and EU terrorism reports suggest that the level of terrorism in Bosnia is no greater than elsewhere in Europe.[27]

On the other hand, a leading Bosnian law enforcement official said that the only reason there have not been more terrorist attacks was that "We've had more luck than brains."[28] The actual number of individuals involved is not trivial; Almir Džuvo, the director of the Intelligence and Security Agency of BiH (OSA), estimated in July 2010 that there were 3,000 potential terrorists in Bosnia, out of a population of just under four million people.[29]

Two conclusions can be drawn from these assessments. First, the level of terrorist activity in Bosnia does appear comparable to levels elsewhere in Europe—although, if the Bosnian official cited above is right, any optimism should be guarded at best. Second, just because the terrorist threat is not unusual does not mean it is not necessarily unimportant. Comparisons with Western Europe can be misleading, as terrorism is much more dangerous to a fragile state than to a robust democracy.

Wahhabis.

One *mujahideen* leader predicted in 1996 that "[f]oreign fighters will not be a problem for Bosnia. They will move on. But we planted a seed here and you will have more and more Bosnian Muslims practicing traditional Islam."[30] The most obvious sign of this trend are the so-called Wahhabis, adherents of the fundamentalist Islam practiced in Saudi Arabia.

Estimates of the numbers of Wahhabis or members of similar sects vary widely. Observers were surprised by the crowd of more than 3,000 people, half of them Bosnians, who attended the funeral of a Wahhabist leader in 2007,[31] as well as by a 2013 conference in Tuzla that drew 500 participants, mostly young men.[32] Given that an estimated 4,000 people gather each Friday to hear radical sermons preached at the Saudi-backed King Fahd Mosque in Sarajevo,[33] the number of Wahhabis could be quite high. But the most likely figure is that given by Federation police (not the police of the Serb Republic), who estimated in 2009 that there were up to 5,000 practicing Bosnian Wahhabis.[34]

Unsurprisingly, the Wahhabis recruit followers from the least privileged classes:

> Bosnian Wahhabis largely target youth with few economic opportunities and [the] downtrodden, both from rural areas. They keenly take advantage of poverty, lack of education and poor social services, offering young people and refugees a variety of opportunities, including jobs, income and fellowship. There have been cases in which new members are paid several hundred euros per month for their loyalty. There is also evidence that members are paid for convincing their wives to wear the hijab in public, among other things.[35]

The Saudi role in this process is extensive. The Saudis financed an extensive mosque-building program after the war, of which the $30-million King Fahd Mosque[36] is only the most visible and influential, and built a parallel religious educational structure to that offered by the official Islamic Community.[37] The Saudis are also believed to fund various Wahhabi groups, to educate young Bosnians in Saudi Arabia, and to send operatives to Bosnia who typically marry Bosnian women and blend into local society.[38]

As the Wahhabi movement has gained momentum, militants have engaged in violent clashes with traditional Bosniaks and sought to impose their standards of behavior on the public. Young and charismatic Wahhabi preachers travel through Western Europe and the Balkans, lecturing and giving sermons; they maintain popular websites full of *jihadist* propaganda and incitement to terror. One prominent preacher is known for a pro-*jihadist*, anti-American song that he performs at weddings and other social events:

American and other adversaries should know
That now the Muslims
Are one like the Taliban
Listen, brothers,
Believers of the world
With dynamite on their chest
Lead the path to dzennet (heaven).[39]

Some Bosniaks have always been anti-American, but the vast majority were openly grateful to the United States for intervening to stop the war and then to keep the peace. No recent polls appear to have measured how these views may have changed. It is, however, unrealistic to expect young people born during or after the war to share that sense of gratitude, or indeed, to expect older people to continue to feel gratitude as the political system imposed at Dayton fails to deliver results.

While Wahhabi violence and proselytization are quite visible, these Islamists are even better known for their separatist enclaves, which function as "no-go-zones." The inhabitants of these enclaves reject the authority of the Bosnian government and instead impose a strict interpretation of *sharia*. The first such enclave was in the village of Bocinja Donja, formerly a Bosnian Serb village, where the Bosniak government settled former *mujahideen* after the war.

The *mujahideen* married Bosnian women and so acquired Bosnian citizenship. The village provided them a safe haven in which to maintain their terrorist contacts under the guise of simple farmers. In the 1990s, the hostility of the inhabitants of Bocinja Donja to outsiders, including SFOR, was palpable, undermining their claims of innocence. Eventually the enclave was closed down, and the village returned to its original owners. Now the best-known enclave is in Gornja Maoča, a remote village where native Bosnians reside along with foreign-born former *mujahideen*.

While the Bosnian Serbs continue to insist that these enclaves pose a significant security risk, Bosniak policy has been bifurcated. One the one hand, there has been pressure to isolate and marginalize the Wahhabis, in the hope of making any problems go away. Analyst Stephen Schwartz speculates that Bosniak political leaders have "pursued a strategy of trying to confine the Wahhabi agitators to remote locations, rather than settling the problem by consequential legal proceedings."[40] Not all Bosniak officials are willing to settle for this approach, however. The authorities have made numerous arrests, including a massive 2010 raid on Gornja Maoča and the arrests of two of the enclave's leaders following the 2011 attack on the U.S. embassy in Sarajevo. Up to now, though, they have failed to obtain an indictment, let alone a conviction. As a result, a cloud of mystery is likely to cloak Gornja Maoča and other similar enclaves for some time to come, making it difficult to determine the degree of danger they pose to Bosnia's internal security or their potential links to international terrorism.

Some observers caution that many Wahhabis are peaceful and should not be classified as terrorists, for fear of driving them into the arms of groups espousing violence.[41] The Islamic Community, the official Muslim religious organization in Bosnia, has refused to condemn the Wahhabis and attacks those who criticize them. But the Bosniak public remains unpersuaded; when last asked, 71 percent rejected Wahhabism, suggesting that this form of Islam remains for them both distinct from traditional Bosnian Islam and unwelcome.[42]

The Wahhabis do not yet appear to have gained control of any significant governmental or official religious offices. Nor, although actual numbers are hard to estimate, have they created no-go zones in urban areas, as has happened in Western Europe. This lack of progress is most likely due to visceral opposition from local Bosniaks. Attempts to take over mosques have ended in violence; in one instance, a resident commented: "They should shave their beards and use deodorant instead of coming here like dogs. For me, they are wolf-dogs, they will attack our children. I have female children and do not dare to send them to [the religious school] at all."[43] These locals' contempt of the Wahhabis is unmistakable.

Yet, current descriptions of the Federation suggest it is much more radicalized than was the case in the late-1990s. Given that the trend is pointing in the wrong direction, it would be foolish to regard Wahhabism as purely marginal, especially when an expert like Sarajevo professor Rešid Hafizović describes it as a "potentially deadly virus" for Bosnian Muslims.[44] When times are hard and the future is bleak, such movements can gain momentum quickly.

ISLAMIST TIES OF SENIOR BOSNIAK LEADERS

Islamists are active not only in Bosnia, but throughout Western Europe and the United States. One factor that makes them a greater danger in Bosnia than elsewhere, though, is their close connection to Bosniak leaders, in particularly three men (Bakir Izetbegović, Haris Silajdžić, and Alija Izetbegović). These men have occupied the Bosniak chair of the central state's rotating presidency since its establishment. The danger of the Islamists in Bosnia has also been increased by their closeness to Mustafa Cerić, the mufti who until recently headed Bosnia's official Islamic Community.

Those men, along with their associates and subordinates, have pursued policies inimical to the views and goals of moderate Muslims, and those of Bosnian Serbs and Croats. They have supported Islamist terrorism and Wahhabism, encouraged alienation between Bosniaks and other Bosnians, and sought closer ties with Islamist countries like Saudi Arabia and Iran.

Bakir Izetbegović.

The most prominent Bosniak official today is Bakir Izetbegović, the current Bosniak member of the Presidency of Bosnia and Herzegovina.[45] Bakir served during the war as personal assistant and advisor to his father, Alija Izetbegović, who was then President of Bosnia. After the war, from 1999 to 2003, Bakir was a member of the managing board of the humanitarian Islamic charity, Merhamet. Like other Islamic charities, Merhamet used its humanitarian work as a cover during the war to deliver weapons to Bosnia.[46]

It is unlikely that Izetbegović, as a personal assistant to the President, would have been unaware of these activities. Nor could he have been unaware of the initiative to bring *mujahideen* into Bosnia. In fact, Dževad Galijašević, a former Party of Democratic Action (SDA) official, in 2008, accused Izetbegović of being one of the chief protectors of the *mujahideen* who remained in Bosnia after the war.[47]

Bakir, who for years directed the Construction Bureau of Sarajevo Canton, was involved in the construction of the King Fahd Mosque and reportedly arranged for the land on which the complex was built, previously owned by Serbs, to be donated to the Saudis.[48] This mosque, the largest house of worship for Muslims in the Balkans, is also known for its key role as the center of Wahhabi influence and power in Bosnia.[49] As such, it represents the antithesis of the moderate Islam traditionally practiced in Bosnia. Izetbegović's connection to the mosque suggests that he does not share the antipathy of many of his fellow Bosniaks for the type of Islam that it propagates.

Another indication of Bakir's ideological orientation comes from his involvement in a secular initiative to advance the observance of *sharia*, a key Islamist goal and one that is vehemently opposed by moderate Bosniaks. He was responsible for coordinating the construction of the Bosna Bank International (BBI)

Center in Sarajevo, described as "the only commercial shopping mall in Bosnia and Herzegovina that has prohibited sales of pork and alcohol."[50] The BBI Center was built by the BBI, the only bank in Bosnia to offer *sharia*-compliant finance.[51] Among the principal goals of *sharia*-compliant finance is enhancing the appeal of an Islamic political order. Another is to generate funds that can be used to advance Islamist goals.[52]

Finally, Bakir Izetbegović is known for his sympathies toward Iran. During his tenure in the BiH presidency, bilateral ties between Bosnia and Iran have expanded, including in trade and investment.[53] Izetbegović called for even closer Iranian-Bosnian ties during a meeting with then Iranian president Mahmoud Ahmadinejad in February 2013 in Cairo, Egypt, on the margins of an Organization of Islamic Cooperation (OIC) meeting.[54] While a small country like Bosnia naturally seeks to maintain good ties with powerful countries, these initiatives stand out, coming as they did at a time when the UN, the United States, and the EU have put sanctions in place to isolate the regime in Tehran.

Some of those connections are particularly controversial. The Sarajevo weekly *Slobodna Bosna* reported that, according to the Iranian opposition, the Iranian Ibn Sina Institute in Sarajevo, described as a scientific research institute, is, in fact, the IRGC's headquarters in the Balkans. The magazine also questioned the bona fides of some 200 Iranian "businessmen" who entered Bosnia in the first half of 2012, noting that they appeared to lack business contacts.[55]

The controversy only grows when official Iranians are alleged to have connections to Islamist terrorism. In the spring of 2013, Bakir became embroiled in a dispute with Bosniak political rival Fahrudin Radončić, a former businessman who is currently the state-level minister of security.[56] Bakir reportedly intervened to oppose expelling two Iranian diplomats whom Radončić had accused of improper activities and declared *personae non grata*.[57] The diplomats eventually left, and a third was expelled in June 2013.[58] Two of the three had reportedly made contact with the Wahhabist leader in Gornja Maoča.[59] While no one has alleged any direct contact between Izetbegović and the Iranian diplomats, or between him and the enclave of Gornja Maoča, the reports do raise questions about whether Bosnia's most senior Bosniak politician is opening the door to Iranian intelligence services and terrorist operatives.

Haris Silajdzić.

Izetbegović's predecessor in the tri-presidency was Haris Silajdzić. A prominent SDA politician, Silajdzić was a former close associate of Alija Izetbegović and a senior member of his wartime cabinet, serving first as foreign minister and then as prime minister. During that time, he also oversaw directly the effort to bring *mujahideen* to Bosnia.[60] Silajdzić was an effective spokesman for the Bosniak cause, making the case that his side was Western, secular, and democratic. However, his true convictions apparently lay with the *mujahideen*: In July 1995, he declared an Islamic holy war on Sarajevo TV and invited all Islamic states to fight on the side of Bosnia's Muslims.[61]

After the war, Silajdzić's political career took several twists and turns. He continued to hold high government positions, but in 1997, he left the SDA to form the Party of Bosnia and Herzegovina. He resigned his government and party positions abruptly on September 21, 2001, reportedly because of his radical connections,[62] but remerged 5 years later to win the election to the tri-presidency.

In 2006, Silajdzić ran on a platform to abolish the Federation and the Serb Republic entities and strengthen the central Bosnian state—an unacceptable proposal for any official of the Serb Republic. In office, he engaged in a very public and polarizing dispute with Bosnian Serb leader Milorad Dodik, thereby contributing to the radicalization of Bosnian society. In the opinion of analyst Steven Oluic, Silajdzić took Bosnian society and politics back to the painful days of 1995. It is also noteworthy that the Iranian government not only expressed pleasure at his election but pledged him its continuing support.[63] In 2008, Silajdzić was among those identified by Galijašević as one of the chief Bosnian protectors of the *mujahideen* since the war.[64] Looking at all these factors, there can be little doubt of Silajdžić's Islamist convictions, despite his ability to appeal to Western audiences as a secularist democrat supposedly committed to multi-nationalism.[65]

Alija Izetbegović.

Neither of those men, however, has had as lasting an impact on Bosnian politics and society as Alija Izetbegović, Bakir's father. Izetbegović, the man affectionately called "Dedo" (Grandpa) by many Bosniaks,[66] was Bosnia's president during the war and then the first Bosniak member of the tri-presidency. Throughout, he became the embodiment and symbol of embattled Muslims. Many U.S. policymakers considered him a leading proponent of multiethnic democracy and tolerance. Yet, Izetbegović left numerous signs pointing to his Islamist ideology. Even more importantly, he succeeded in forming an Islamist cadre of insiders, including Haris Silajdzić and Bakir Izetbegović, which remains highly influential today and has done much to shape Bosnia's post-war history.

Izetbegović's Islamist ideology is laid out in his famous political manifesto, The *Islamic Declaration*,[67] for which, during the 1980s, he was sentenced to 5 years in prison.[68] Some excerpts, shown in Box 2, provide disturbing insights into his thinking.

Box 2

The *Islamic Declaration* on Islamic Government and Society.

- . . . the Islamic order posits two fundamental assumptions: an Islamic society and Islamic governance. . . . An Islamic society without an Islamic authority is incomplete and without power; Islamic governance without an Islamic society is either utopia or violence (p. 26).
- There can be neither peace nor coexistence between the Islamic religion and non-Islamic social and political institutions (p. 30).
- . . . the Islamic movement should and can start to take over power as soon as it is morally and numerically strong enough to be able to overturn not only the existing non-Islamic government, but also to build up a new Islamic one. . . . (p. 56).

Simply put, Muslims living in a non-Muslim majority country should play by the rules of that country—until they are strong enough to overthrow the system and install an Islamic government. Nothing in the *Declaration* suggested any compromise toward this goal.

Most Westerners ignored the *Declaration* or dismissed its contents on the assumption that it had been attacked by the Yugoslav government simply because it was an anti-communist tract. But the *Declaration* was much more than that—and it was politically relevant after the fall of Yugoslavia. It was published in 1990 (before that, it was distributed secretly only)[69] and later distributed to the troops of the Bosniak army.[70] Since then, the *Declaration* has figured prominently in Bosniak-Serb political disputes. Bosnian Serb leaders Radovan Karadzić and Milorad Dodik have both testified before the International Criminal Tribunal for the Former Yugoslavia (ICTY) in The Hague, The Czech Republic, that Izetbegović intended to build an Islamic state in Bosnia based on the concepts set out in the *Declaration*.[71]

Accusations of Izetbegović's continued commitment to the ideology of the *Declaration* were consistent with his marked preference for the Islamist regime in Iran. That preference first surfaced in 1983, when he was accused of seeking Iranian support for his cause.[72] Izetbegović visited Iran in May 1991 as president of Bosnia and obtained assurances of Iranian support a year prior to the outbreak of hostilities.[73] His heavy reliance on Iran during the war presumably reinforced his view of the Iranian Islamist regime as a genuine ally. This positive view of Iran, as shown previously, appears to be shared by his son, Bakir.

Ideology is, of course, of little impact without an organization to implement it. Izetbegović created such an organization in the late-1980s: the SDA. Although the SDA gave the impression of being a moderate Muslim party in order to win Bosniak votes and garner Western sympathy, its inner core was comprised of former Young Muslims.[74] The Young Muslims was the conspiratorial group, patterned after the Muslim Brotherhood, which Izetbegović had joined in 1941. It based its operations and program on Islamism,[75] and one of its main principles was the unification of the Muslim world through the creation of a large Muslim state.[76]

Although the Yugoslav government did its best to stamp out the group, it survived underground for decades. Some of its leading members (Hasan Čengić, Omer Behmen, Edhem Bičakčić, Huso Zivalj, and Ismet Kasumagic), imprisoned with Izetbegović in 1983, were assigned the most sensitive and important tasks during the war. Hasan Čengić, for example, sat on the board of directors of the Third World Relief Agency (TWRA). TWRA was the principal conduit for sending money (much of it from Iran) and arms to Bosnia.[77] Omer Behmen handled SDA personnel matters[78] before working the other end of the pipeline as ambassador to Iran. Muhammed Sacirbey, Izetbegović's wartime ambassador to the UN, was the son of Nedžib Šaeirbegović who had been imprisoned with Izetbegović after World War II.[79] Nedžib was appointed ambassador-at-large to Islamic countries.[80]

Several Young Muslims continued their political careers in the post-war period: Zivalj became Bosnia's ambassador to the UN, and Bičakčić became prime minister of the Federation. After the war, Čengić served as Federation deputy defense minister until the

United States forced his dismissal.[81] Behmen focused on ideology, working actively with Islamist youth organizations and educational institutions on a so-called "third offensive" of the Young Muslims movement.[82]

The fortunes of most of these individuals have attracted little attention from U.S. policymakers, but the same cannot be said for the activity that first drew Western attention to Izetbegović's Islamist connections: his decision to bring *mujahideen* to Bosnia. His personal connections reached the very top of al-Qaeda: during the war Osama Bin Laden, who had been issued a Bosnian passport, reportedly met Izetbegović in his Sarajevo office.[83]

After the war, all foreign fighters were required to leave Bosnia under the terms of the Dayton Peace Accords. Despite the best efforts of IFOR and the U.S. Government, many still remained in the country — and Izetbegović protected them. He openly supported supposedly disbanded *mujahideen* military units,[84] while numerous murders and other acts of violence, particularly against Bosnian Croats living in the Federation, were carried out by those same *mujahideen* and their Bosnian accomplices.[85]

These were not just random acts of violence in a lawless post-war period. Rather, the SDA was using the *mujahideen* "as powerful leverage in a struggle to maintain an ethnic majority in previously mixed regions of Central Bosnia and Sarajevo. . . ."[86] In the process, Bosnia itself became the victim: Independent Bosniak journalist Senad Avdić reportedly accused the party of turning the country into "a European dump for all kinds of scum, murderers, terrorists, and adventurers of all sorts who have earned the status of equal citizens of this country with 'selam' and 'tekbir'."[87]

During the same period, more than 200 Iranian agents reportedly infiltrated Bosniak political and social circles as well as the U.S. "Train and Equip" military program, collaborating closely with a pro-Iranian faction within the Bosniak intelligence service. These agents aimed to gather information, sow dissension between Bosniak and Croat participants in "Train and Equip," and turn Bosniak leaders against the West. It is highly unlikely that Izetbegović was unaware of this activity, as the Bosniak intelligence service at that time reported directly to him.[88]

In the aftermath of the terrorist attacks of 9/11, a number of terrorists were apprehended, and the charities funding them were closed. Then moderate political parties won a national election, and Munir Alibabić, a senior Bosniak security expert known for opposing al-Qaeda and the Iranian influence, was appointed head of the Federation Intelligence and Security Service.[89]

In May 2002, Alibabić arrested five senior Bosniak officials connected to the SDA on suspicion of terrorism and espionage. The officials were allegedly linked to the murders of Croats, bomb blasts at Catholic sites, and two high-profile assassinations. The SDA protested; all were released in October 2002, and no indictment was ever brought.[90] Instead, Alibabić was dismissed by OHR's High Representative Paddy Ashdown for mishandling intelligence information.[91]

The SDA soon returned to power, making revelations of its misdeeds even more unlikely, while at the same time, the accusations fester and suspicions remain regarding their Islamist sympathies. As one analyst wrote, "There are countless examples of local authorities in Bosnia failing to act properly against Islamic extremism. The majority of these criminal cases have not been resolved and when the terrorists are identified the trials take years."[92] The SDA top leadership may be innocent of the charges leveled against it, but it has made no effort to clear the air.

Much about Izetbegović's wartime activities might have become known had he lived longer: At the time of his death in 2003, the ICTY was investigating him for alleged war crimes. However, after he died, the ICTY closed its investigation, thus shutting off a major avenue of inquiry that might have illuminated some of these murky postwar terrorist activities.

Mustafa Cerić.

Much of the support for Bosniak nationalist parties and policies comes from former Grand Mufti of Sarajevo Mustafa Cerić. For years, he led the Islamic Community, the official Muslim organization in Bosnia. Despite his position in a religious hierarchy, Cerić "has been and is playing an increasingly important political role among Bosniaks, that often surpasses that of any politician," according to a Bosnian human rights advocate.[93] Like Silajdzić, Cerić set himself up in opposition to Dodik, continuing wartime rhetoric by portraying Bosniaks as victims in mortal danger from the Serbs.

Feted in Western Europe as a moderate Muslim, Cerić enjoys a different reputation at home, where he is known as "homo duplex," the man with two faces. This nickname arises from numerous indications that he is anything but "moderate"—a judgment based on his ties to the Muslim Brotherhood, his view regarding the imposition of *sharia*, and his positions on Wahhabism. These range from refusing to condemn it to hurling accusations of Islamophobia at anyone who criticizes it.

Cerić's current ties to the Muslim Brotherhood arise from his membership in two pan-European organizations: the European Council for Research and Fatwa, a Brotherhood-linked group chaired by Sheikh Yousef al-Qaradawi, the spiritual leader of the Brotherhood, and the UK-based "Radical Middle Way," which includes a wide range of scholars associated with the global Muslim Brotherhood.[94]

On several occasions, Cerić has publicly advocated positions consistent with Brotherhood ideology. For example, in 2006, he issued the document, "A Declaration of European Muslims," in which he declared European Muslims (including Bosniaks) fully committed to the values of democracy and human rights but called, among other things, for the partial implementation of *sharia*.[95] Several years later he argued, in a speech in Berlin, Germany, that implementing *sharia* would not be contrary to Bosnia's constitution — a position that would probably surprise most Bosniaks.[96]

Over the years, Cerić has refused to condemn Wahhabism. His position stands in stark contrast to that of representatives and leaders of the Islamic Community in Montenegro, who did not hesitate to condemn Wahhabist activities.[97] Cerić has implied that his stance simply reflects his relative weakness. The King Fahd Mosque and many other religious institutions funded by the Saudis who spread Wahhabism are not under the control of the Islamic Community. When asked if Saudi funding was deleterious, Cerić replied that Bosnia was in no position to turn down money from Saudi Arabia, which, after all, was an ally of the West.[98]

But Cerić goes far beyond what would be required if he were simply bowing to a stronger player. He attacks critics of Wahhabism for being "Islamophobes" (a well-known, if poorly-defined, term coined by the

Muslim Brotherhood), and has led the way in developing the concept of "good" versus "bad" Bosniaks.

As the Embassy in Sarajevo reported in a 2009 classified cable released by Wikileaks:

> 'Good Bosniaks,' according to this sentiment, are those who espouse conservative political and religious ideals. More moderate and secular ideals are, by implication, held by 'bad Bosniaks.' Statements from the Islamic Community, particularly its leader, [Grand Mufti] Cerić, that label those who criticize Islamic Community as 'Islamophobic' have sharpened this polarization among Bosniaks.[99]

Indeed, in 2010 and 2011, the Islamic Community issued reports on Islamophobia, cataloguing all the statements and actions that it believes express intolerance, hate, and hostility against Islam and Muslims. The definition deliberately obscures any differences among Muslims.[100]

In 2012, Cerić was replaced as Grand Mufti by Hussein Effendi Kavazović, the mufti of Tuzla who is considered close to Cerić.[101] The well-known observer group, International Crisis Group (ICG), recently suggested that "[t]he Islamic community's best contribution would be to help craft a vision for Bosnia that Croats and Serbs can share."[102] The Islamic Community, after years of Cerić's leadership, has a long way to go to address the Islamism in its midst. Until that happens, the Community is unlikely to produce a unifying vision that all Bosnians can support.

In fact, the long-term impact of the Islamism of these men and their colleagues, subordinates, and supporters will most likely be extremely detrimental to the future of the country. Bosniak terror expert Dževad Galijašević describes the danger vividly:

Active Islamism is pushing one's own nation in the whirlpool of problems of other Islamic countries. It is getting Bosnian Muslims interested in events in the Arab world, in the Iranian revolution, in the Islamic Republic of Pakistan. It is bringing Bosnia closer to Palestine. It is turning Muslims' true historical brothers, Serbs and Croats, into eternal and irreconcilable enemies, and turning Arabs into the only and actual brothers who look, behave, and talk differently and have a completely different view of the family, the state, and themselves.[103]

The following section examines in more detail the way in which Islamism promotes alienation among Bosnian ethnic groups.

ISLAMISM AND INTER-ETHNIC TENSIONS

Analysts often blame the failure to build a Bosnian state on the Serbs and Croats. Certainly, members of both ethnic groups have contributed to that failure, in part by their own actions and in part because of the external "pull" from a neighboring state. Croatia offers Bosnian Croats refuge in a country that is becoming Western, joining NATO and the EU, and achieving prosperity—unlike Bosnia—and some Croats have already left. Bosnian Serbs have not been so lucky: Serbia and the vision of Greater Serbia are languishing in the political, economic, and social doldrums. Yet, Serbia was once an economic powerhouse, and even today Bosnian Serbs dream about reuniting the Serb Republic with it, regardless of any practical difficulties.

It is wrong, however, to disregard the "push" factors (aside from the poor economy) that also exert a powerful influence on Bosnian Serbs and Croats. One very important factor is embedded in Balkan history during the period when the Ottoman Empire enforced *sharia*. *Sharia* covers all aspects of life, not just religious doctrine and practice, and applies to non-Muslims as well as to Muslims. It grants Islam a privileged, protected status, and conflicts directly with Western concepts such as freedom of speech and religion and universal human rights. There is no equality before the law; for example, men have more rights than women, and Muslims have more rights than non-Muslims. Non-Muslims are not allowed to rule over Muslims.[104]

Under the Ottomans, in accordance with *sharia*, non-Muslims were "tolerated;" that is, they were allowed to maintain their religious communities and laws but enjoyed fewer rights than Muslims in a system now referred to as *dhimmitude*. The presence of non-Muslims was tolerated as long as they played by the rules. Failure to do so meant that they were no longer protected and could be killed.[105]

Bosnian Serbs and Croats have not forgotten this system of *dhimmitude*. When Bosniak politicians talk about tolerance, Serbs and Croats suspect that they really mean a political system in which Muslims dominate. Similarly, Serbs and Croats dismiss Bosniak leaders' affirmations of their commitment to multiethnicity, since under *sharia*, "multiethnic" means that many different ethnicities co-exist peacefully — but only under Muslim domination and according to strict rules.

These tensions would exist to some degree, regardless of which political ideology was dominant among Bosniaks. As historian Aleksa Djilas described the problem in 1992:

Muslims imagined Bosnia as an independent state in which they would predominate. Although it was only Muslim extremists who thought non-Muslims should be expelled from Bosnia, most Muslim leaders believed only a Muslim should be allowed full citizenship. Religious Muslims based their demand for supremacy on the traditional belief that the rule of non-Muslims over Muslims was blasphemous. But most Muslims were typical nationalists. They wanted more for their group. . . .[106]

Islamists do, in fact, hold more extreme views than do traditional Muslims regarding the treatment of non-Muslims. The results are obvious in numerous countries today where the Muslim Brotherhood, along with other Islamist groups, has contributed greatly to the destruction of property, torture, murder, and mass migration of non-Muslims from lands where they had lived for over 1,400 years.

In his *Islamic Declaration*,[107] Alija Izetbegović, took a less extreme position regarding non-Muslims, but one that nevertheless provides no comfort to Bosnian Serbs and Croats. The *Declaration*'s message is simple: Muslims should play by the democratic rules until they are strong enough to impose an Islamic state. Once there is an Islamic state, non-Muslims may remain, but only in a subordinate status. If Christians abandoned their religious organization, Izetbegović was prepared to offer them "understanding and cooperation." (See Box 3.)

Box 3
The *Islamic Declaration* on Living with Non-Muslims.

Muslims in a non-Islamic state:
- Muslim minorities within a non-Islamic community, provided they are guaranteed freedom to practice their religion, to live and develop normally, are loyal and must fulfill all their commitments to that community, except those which harm Islam and Muslims (p. 50).
- The position of Muslim minorities in non-Islamic communities will always in reality depend on the strength of the international Islamic community and the esteem in which it is held (p. 50).

Non-Muslim minorities in an Islamic state:
- The non-Muslim minorities within an Islamic state, provided they are loyal, enjoy religious freedom and all protection (p. 50).
- [W]e differentiate between Christ's teaching and the church. The former we regard as the pronunciation of God, deformed on some points, and the latter as an organization, which . . . has become not only non-Islamic, but anti-Christian. (p. 68)
- If Christians so wish, the future may offer an example of understanding and cooperation between two great religions for the well-being of people and mankind (p. 68).

The influence that Islamists hold in Bosnia is also key with regard to their publicly stated goal of establishing a global Caliphate. The Caliphate last existed under the Ottoman Empire. While talking about it may baffle or bemuse Westerners, the reference is all too clear to inhabitants of the Balkans. This Islamist goal is dangerous because it also appeals to non-Islamist Muslims and because it is shared by two increasingly important foreign players: Turkey and the OIC.

The importance of Bosnia to Turkey has been abundantly clear ever since Turkey joined the UN wartime peacekeeping mission there in the 1990s. The Turkish military remained in its headquarters in Zenica after the cessation of hostilities and joined the IFOR/SFOR mission. The military transitioned seamlessly to the EUFOR Althea follow-on mission, where Turkey is now the second largest troop-contributing nation.[108]

In recent years, Turkey has used its relative economic strength to build influence in the Balkans. Its trade with those countries has increased, as has its investment in Bosnia. On the cultural side, Turkish companies have built the largest university campus in the Balkans in Ilidža, a suburb of Sarajevo.[109] These developments are all the more visible, given the absence of increased investment from Europe or the United States. Turkish diplomats have also been very active in seeking to promote reconciliation among the Balkan countries.

Regional conciliation and economic development are laudable goals, and even cultural ties with Turkey are welcomed by many ethnic groups.[110] The nostalgia of Turkish Prime Minister Recep Tayyip Erdoğan and Foreign Minister Ahmet Davutoğlu for the Ottoman Empire, however, is more likely to raise the hackles of non-Muslims.[111] A good example of this is the controversy provoked by remarks that Davutoğlu made at a 2009 Sarajevo conference on "Ottoman Heritage and Muslim Communities in the Balkans Today." His speech was ambiguous: He proclaimed that "[n]ow is the time for reunification" in the form of "reestablishing ownership in the region, through reestablishing multicultural coexistence, and through establishing a new economic zone."[112] He did not specify what he meant by "reunification," nor who the new owner would be, but he clearly meant Turkey to dominate. For those Bosnians who put Davutoğlu's remarks in a historical context, his call for "multicultural coexistence" was likely to be interpreted as a reference to the Ottoman system of *dhimmitude*. Nor was it much more helpful to place the remarks in a modern context, given that Christians feel increasingly endangered in an even-more "Islamist" Turkey.[113]

Turkish "neo-Ottomanism" in itself is unlikely to become a credible threat to Bosnians, since the American Embassy in Ankara described Turkey as having "Rolls Royce ambitions, but Rover resources."[114] But the topic itself remains sensitive. Were the Bosniak leadership genuinely committed to reconciling Bosnia's ethnic groups, it would presumably find some diplomatic way to cushion or rebut such statements.

In addition to its bilateral ties to Turkey, Saudi Arabia, and Iran, Bosnia has observer status at the OIC, the international organization representing 56 Muslim countries and the Palestinian Authority. Saudi Arabia provides the most funding for the OIC; Iran, Pakistan, Malaysia, Indonesia, and Turkey are other leading members. While not an Islamist organization, the OIC is dedicated to advancing Islam throughout the world and to supporting Muslim minorities in non-Islamic countries. It shares the vision of a global Caliphate that implements *sharia* and, indeed, claims to be its present embodiment.[115] From time to time, OIC members may be at odds with the Muslim Brotherhood, but both organizations nevertheless cooperate to promote mutual objectives.

During an April 2013 visit to Sarajevo, OIC Secretary General Ekmeleddin İhsanoğlu urged Bosnia to upgrade to full membership. Bakir Izetbegović suggested that full membership would be useful to Bosnia by giving it access to OIC development funding.[116] Were this to occur, Bosnia would presumably have to adopt any existing OIC agreements or conventions, including the 1990 Cairo Declaration on Human Rights.[117] The Cairo Declaration rules out any rights incompatible with the *Koran*. That principle negates much of Western human rights, such as equality for religious minorities and freedom of speech, including the right to criticize Islam.

The OIC reinforces the tenets of the Cairo Declaration by means of annual reports on Islamophobia in Western countries, similar to the reports on Bosnia prepared by the Islamic Community. Bosnian OIC membership would probably give added impetus to this exercise, making it ever more difficult to criticize Islamist policies or groups. The OIC could be expected to show an active interest in Bosnian internal developments, as it recently resuscitated its Bosnia Contact Group from the early-1990s.[118] There is little chance that the OIC would remain neutral regarding disputes between Bosniaks and Bosnian Serbs and Croats.

Given all these factors, Bakir Izetbegović's comments in favor of full OIC membership were hardly designed to improve inter-ethnic relations. Bosnian Serbs and Croats may exaggerate the threat of Islamism or potential Islamic dominance, but the Bosniak leadership certainly provides them with plenty of ammunition.

POTENTIAL SOURCES OF VIOLENCE

Many observers worry that the situation in Bosnia could spiral downward into violence, and call for Western intervention, whether political or military, to ward off such a development. This section reviews potential sources of destabilizing violence as a prelude to discussing Western options.

Few observers think that renewed inter-ethnic tension could lead to the level of violence that occurred in the early-1990s. Partly, this is because, as detailed previously, the impetus in Serbia or Croatia to fuel a civil war or to intervene directly is greatly reduced from what it was 2 decades ago.

Moreover, Bosnian military forces have undergone significant change. In 2006, the armies of the three "former warring factions" were melded into a unified Armed Forces of Bosnia and Herzegovina (AFBiH) under a central ministry of defense, and radically downsized. The force has a mandated strength of 10,000 professional soldiers, with a reserve of 5,000, and 1,000 civilian employees. According to a 2011 study, actual troops are estimated to be only 8,500, of which an estimated 2,000 troops are required to guard defense sites containing arms and munitions. The reserves are inactive. Lack of funding constrains the army's efforts to meet NATO standards and to contribute troops to NATO missions.[119]

The AFBiH, although small in size, is courted in today's highly politicized environment. The 2011 study reported "numerous incidents . . . of political leaders addressing AFBiH officers and troops with nationalist statements at events with nationalist symbols, including politicians from neighboring states."[120] However, few think that the ethnically integrated command structure is likely to do anything rash. Rather, "[t]he general fear is not that the AFBiH will **generate** instability, but rather that it could fall victim to deepening political instability."[121]

During and after the war, the separate secret police structures of the three ethnic groups were responsible for much mayhem and havoc. Today, they have, at least formally, been dismantled and their functions taken over since 2004 by the OSA. The OSA is charged with intelligence gathering to protect the security, territorial integrity, and constitutional order of Bosnia.[122]

OSA has been praised for its professional conduct and political independence.[123] Unfortunately, it must share its responsibility for pursuing organized crime with the regular police forces and the judiciary, who remain more vulnerable to political pressure and corruption.[124] In the polarized atmosphere of recent years, there is little chance this will change. OSA must also share its duty to combat terrorism with many other agencies. While Bosnia has made overall progress in this area, occasional lapses such as the mysterious disappearance from prison of the well-known terrorist Karay Kamel bin Ali, aka Abu Hamza, still occur.[125]

If Bosnia's neighbors and its armed forces appear unlikely to initiate ethnic violence, that does not mean there is no threat. The authors of the 2011 security study cited previously, worry about the possibility of lower-level violence, which will most likely coalesce along ethnic lines. People who could be drawn into such violence include members of various domestic groups like football hooligans, special forces, and intelligence veterans now employed by private security companies, or individuals in the police forces and judiciary — two key institutions in which reforms to establish professionalism and impartiality remain incomplete.[126] Such violence, while short of war, could nevertheless be devastating to regular, law-abiding Bosnians.

THE U.S. POLICY ENVIRONMENT

For most Americans, the Balkans faded from view a decade ago, and Bosnia is a long-forgotten, remote place of no particular interest. At the time, however, the Bill Clinton administration and much of the foreign policy elite feted making and keeping the peace in Bosnia as a significant foreign policy achievement. The George H. W. Bush administration, initially skeptical, maintained the SFOR mission and then terminated it successfully. This success contrasts with the disillusionment over subsequent U.S. missions in Iraq and Afghanistan.

Indeed, there was reason to celebrate. Conditions in Bosnia remained largely peaceful throughout the 9 years of IFOR/SFOR deployment: SFOR retained its authority, kept casualties to a minimum, and helped bring about significant defense and military reforms. When SFOR departed in 2004, the handover to EUFOR was not only orderly and peaceful, but welcomed by the EU. It was not until 2 years after SFOR's departure that Bosnia's political environment began to unravel.

Geopolitically, there is much to be said for seeking to ensure that Bosnia retains its territorial integrity and Western orientation—that, like most other European countries, it joins both NATO and the EU. Yet, today, these desired outcomes are far from assured. Calls for a third, Croat entity or other forms of Croat separatism threaten the current fragile political balance within the Federation. Russia has courted the

Bosnian Serbs as they call for secession and/or a referendum on NATO accession,[127] and the OIC has done the same with the Bosniaks. Were Bosnia to split into three parts, the Bosniak rump state would come under strong pressure to join the OIC and could, in so doing, set a decidedly non-Western course.

The Europeans are as mindful of these risks as are the Americans, but the EU's recent experiences have made them very pessimistic about what outsiders can do if Bosnians refuse to help themselves. In addition, the EU is preoccupied with urgent problems of its own, such as the recurring euro crisis.

Nor is the EU equipped to resolve Bosnia's interethnic tensions. On such issues, fuzzy rhetoric prevails, not constructive policies or actions. For example, EU Council President Herman Van Rompuy, in response to a complaint by Bosnian Croat Cardinal Vinko Puljić that Bosnian Muslim discrimination was driving out Catholics, countered that a "European perspective" (e.g., EU membership) "is the only way to overcome the crisis."[128] Exactly how this transformation would work is unclear, especially since the European Commission, in its 2012 annual report on Bosnia, devoted one short paragraph out of 60 pages to the issue of religious discrimination—and offered a high-level interfaith meeting as a remedy.[129]

Puljić had linked the tension between Muslims and Catholics to the growth of Islamism, arguing that "[t]ime is running out as there is a worrisome rise in radicalism." Yet, the Bosnian government has done more than its EU counterparts to combat Islamism. No EU government has conducted a raid like the one in 2010 on the Wahhabist village of Gornja Maoča, despite the growth in various West European cities of similar, *sharia*-implementing enclaves.

Instead, EU governments categorize these areas as no-go zones and advise non-Muslims to avoid them. They appear to have no plan for keeping *sharia* zones from undermining the democratic rule of law in their countries or from incubating or protecting terrorists. Expecting the EU to solve Bosnia's current problems tied to Islamism is simply unrealistic.

MILITARY OPTIONS

Given the deteriorating conditions in Bosnia, some have called for the United States to reassert leadership there before violence breaks out again. Two proposals by experts on Bosnia are worth examining: first, for a new military mission, and second, for accelerated Bosnian entry into NATO.

A New Military Mission.

Janusz Bugajski of the Center for Strategic and International Studies argues that ground forces must be deployed to avert violence. Unlike IFOR/SFOR, European nations should assume primary responsibility, while the United States provides "strong diplomatic, political, and logistical support." The exercise would be backed by "a firmer trans-Atlantic strategic commitment to bringing all countries in the region into both NATO and the EU."[130]

Bugajski's proposal assumes that an international military force would not only forestall violence, but return Bosnia to a path of reform that would allow it to join NATO and the EU. However, hopes that a military mission could restart reforms appear to be based on a misreading of the past. SFOR and NATO's follow-on military headquarters in Sarajevo were, indeed, instrumental in pushing for a unified Bosnian military, one of the major post-Dayton achievements. SFOR, however, had the authority to weigh in on defense sector reforms because military oversight fell within its purview under Annex 1A of the Dayton Peace Accords.

It is by no means clear why another military mission would succeed in putting Bosnia back on track to join either organization. The stumbling block to NATO accession is purely political: The Bosnian Serbs are not only refusing to transfer military facilities to the central state but have called NATO membership itself into question. It would be suicidal for an international military mission to inject itself into this dispute.

Nor could such a mission help promote EU accession, a far-more-complex and demanding process than NATO accession—covering everything from agriculture to finance to transport—and in which a military mission would have neither authority nor expertise. A military mission by itself is highly unlikely to somehow cajole or force Bosnians back onto the path of reform and nation-building. Although a military mission is unlikely to advance either NATO or EU accession, it could still appear attractive if an outbreak of violence were to threaten the gains made in Bosnia since Dayton. Again, the comparison with IFOR/SFOR could prove misleading on several counts.

First, IFOR/SFOR relied heavily on European troop contributors. Yet, the European experiences in Bosnia since SFOR's departure in 2004 have not been positive. The EU-led EUFOR in Sarajevo has not fared well; it began with 7,000 troops in December 2004 and has since been reduced to a troop level of 600.[131] This reduction reflects its drop in effectiveness. According to Azinovic *et al*, most observers believe that EUFOR's visibility is its only contribution; that its ability to deter politically directed violence is very limited.[132]

In part, this decline is the result of troop requirements for other missions, as EU military forces are also required for NATO, UN, and national military missions. But it has also occurred because the EU political establishment has failed to support EUFOR. For example, in March 2011, the EU Political and Security Committee (PSC), charged with political control and strategic guidance for the mission,[133] simply did not respond when told that EUFOR needed three times the existing force requirement.[134] EUFOR's composition reflects this lack of political commitment: West European countries have already pulled out, leaving Austria, Turkey, Hungary, and Bulgaria as the main troop contributors.

Second, after several painful experiences, SFOR determined that the best units for dealing with low-level violence were paramilitary police or gendarmes (which the United States does not have). These units specialize in subduing civilian crowds like football hooligans and are much better equipped than regular soldiers to deal with "rent-a-mobs" that include women and children, or with other low-level threats encountered in Bosnia. Yet, the EUFOR withdrawals included European gendarmerie forces; today only some Turkish gendarmes remain in EUFOR.[135] Their use against Serb or Croat crowds is probably limited.

Third, the United States cannot expect to project much influence by means of over-the-horizon forces. NATO now provides EUFOR such support; yet that alone is insufficient to boost EUFOR capabilities. Given European "Bosnia fatigue," the inescapable conclusion is that any new mission would most likely have to include U.S. ground troops, of which Army units would be the principal component.

Were U.S. policymakers at some point to contemplate a mission involving U.S. forces, they would need to factor in the increased danger from Islamism, particularly Islamist terrorism. For much of the 9 years of IFOR/SFOR operations in Bosnia, the *mujahideen* were forced into hiding. Izetbegović protected them, but his room for maneuvering was limited both by U.S. policy and by widespread pro-Americanism and anti-Wahhabism among Bosniaks.

Nevertheless, IFOR/SFOR enjoyed only limited success in combating terrorism—unsurprisingly, as it was tasked primarily with maintaining a safe and secure environment. The list of high-profile international plots hatched during and after SFOR's tenure (see Box 1) shows the difficulty a military force with only limited counterterrorist capabilities has in deterring such activity, especially when local officials shield the terrorists from outside pressure.

Today's NATO presence is no better equipped to deal with a terrorist threat. Counterterrorism is not even among the top three missions of the current NATO headquarters in Sarajevo.[136] Nor would preparing Bosnia for NATO membership help, as the accession requirements revolve primarily around issues of democratic legitimacy and defense-sector capabilities.

In addition, Islamist anti-Americanism has now had a chance to put down roots. How deep those roots are is hard to determine, but the possibility of *jihadist* violence against U.S. or Western troops is probably greater than it was previously. Some terrorists would likely be homegrown and able to blend more easily into the native population. Any new mission would have to factor this enhanced threat into its planning.

Shortly before the Dayton Peace Accords and the start of IFOR, General Charles G. Boyd, USAF (Ret.), former deputy commander of the European Command, argued that the United States should give equal weight to the fears and aspirations of Serbs as well as to those of Muslims and Croats. He further argued that military action alone would not bring about a lasting peace.[137] Eighteen years later, his analysis remains relevant. Political disputes are at the base of Bosnia's problems, some of which reflect the destabilizing and deleterious impact of Islamism. Without a policy that addresses such problems, no military mission is likely to succeed.

Accelerated NATO Membership.

Balkan expert Edward P. Joseph wants the United States to refocus on achieving Bosnian membership in NATO rather than the EU, as it is more obtainable. He predicts that accelerated NATO membership would transform the political climate in Bosnia, ending any debate over changes to its territorial integrity.[138] In a similar vein, military expert Steven Oluic writes that "Bosnia's ability to resist extremism and radical Islam depends on continued Western engagement in the region and the recent phenomena of moderate Bosniaks challenging the radical Islamists and their ideologies."[139] Unfortunately, if the West pushes Bosnian Serbs to transfer military facilities to the central state without acknowledging or countering their concerns about Islamism or Muslim dominance, this move is unlikely to succeed and may only increase opposition to NATO.

Bosnia's eventual NATO membership would raise other issues, not only because part of the Bosniak political elite has ties to Islamist groups like the Muslim Brotherhood, but also because Bosnia is openly cultivating closer ties with Iran at a time when the Western world is united in applying sanctions to that country. It is also difficult to predict how Bosnia and other Balkan countries with large Muslim populations and growing Islamist influence will react to future NATO crisis operations in Muslim countries.

RECOMMENDATIONS FOR THE U.S. ARMY

This monograph has laid out in detail arguments against a new military mission in Bosnia. Nevertheless, should U.S. policymakers consider the possibility, the OSD and the JCS should point out the fact that such a mission is unlikely to solve Bosnia's political problems or expedite NATO/EU membership but would instead face serious difficulties. Their analysis could draw on the extensive experience acquired by the U.S. Army during 9 years of IFOR/SFOR deployment in the country, as well as on the expertise gained by participation in the NATO headquarters unit in Sarajevo.

The analysis could include:

- The reasons a military mission would be unlikely to advance Bosnia's accession to NATO. In particular, NATO could hurt the process by putting pressure on the Bosnian Serbs to give more power to a central state they fear will be dominated by Muslims.
- A reminder that IFOR/SFOR and NATO success in unifying the armies of the three ethnic groups and in creating a central ministry of defense occurred in a sector where they had expertise and exercised authority. A new military mission would be unlikely to repeat that success in nonmilitary sectors.

- The difficult experience of our European Allies under the EUFOR and their decision to disengage from Bosnia make it unlikely that they would be willing to provide troops for a new mission.
- The threat of low-level violence and the limited ability of U.S. military troops to combat it make European gendarme forces critical. Yet, those troops are unlikely to be available.
- Security-related developments in the country have deteriorated since SFOR's departure. Anti-Americanism has grown as poorer Bosnians are radicalized by Wahhabis or other Islamist groups, while homegrown Bosnian terrorists as well as former *mujahideen* may threaten U.S. personnel or facilities.

With regard to the expedited entry of Bosnia into NATO, OSD and JCS should ensure that policymakers focus on broader political issues that to date have received insufficient attention, particularly:
- The danger of pushing for a central state that Bosnian Serbs will never accept if they see it as a vehicle to reduce them to the status of second-class citizens in a Muslim-dominated state.
- The danger of sharing classified information and decisionmaking with Bosnian politicians and representatives with ties to the Muslim Brotherhood and Iran.

To prepare for such a debate, the U.S. European Command (EUCOM) and U.S. Army Europe (USAREUR) may wish to retrieve any available in-house expertise and institutional memory on Bosnia, particularly among those who have served or are serving in those commands, as well as those who served on OSD's Balkans Task Force.

Unfortunately, the U.S. military presence in Europe is a shadow of what it was during the IFOR/SFOR mission, and many such individuals have dispersed or been engaged for years in missions in Iraq, Afghanistan, or elsewhere. However, civilian analysts and political advisers, including individuals who served in the NATO headquarters in Sarajevo, may have valuable in-country experience to contribute. In addition, consulting present and past EUFOR participants could prove useful.

ENDNOTES

1. Albania, Bulgaria, Croatia, Romania, and Slovenia have joined NATO, while Bosnia-Herzegovina, Macedonia, Montenegro, and Serbia are members of the Euro-Atlantic Partnership Council. Of these, only Serbia has not indicated a desire to join NATO. Bulgaria, Croatia, Romania, and Slovenia have joined the EU, and Macedonia, Montenegro, and Serbia have been accepted as candidates. Albania and Bosnia-Herzegovina are potential candidates.

2. The United States "remain[s] committed to the Dayton principles of one sovereign and functional Bosnia and Herzegovina comprised of two vibrant entities and Brcko District and based on the equality of three constituent peoples and others." See *sarajevo.usembassy.gov/speech_20130703.html*.

3. Lana Pasic, "Sources of Energy in Bosnia and Herzegovina, and Implications for Energy Security," *Balkananalysis.com*, May 9, 2011.

4. Boris Divjak and Michael Pugh, "The Political Economy of Corruption in Bosnia and Herzegovina," *International Peacekeeping*, Vol. 15, No. 3, June 2008, pp. 373-386.

5. "Improving Opportunities for Young People in Bosnia Herzegovina," *World Bank* website, February 14, 2013.

6. "Ante Markovic's testimony," *Novi List*, October 24, 2003.

7. Ajdin Kamber, "Segregated Bosnian Schools Reinforce Ethnic Division," *Institute for War & Peace Reporting*, May 3, 2011.

8. Morton Abramowitz and James Hooper, "The Death of the Bosnian State," *The National Interest*, July 20, 2011. The next census was held in October 2013. The State Department's 2012 report on religious freedom cites a higher number, 15 percent, based on information from Bosnian statistical authorities. See *www.ecoi.net/local_link/247588/357813_en.html*.

9. "Focus on Bosnia Herzegovina," *Gallup Balkan Monitor*, GMB Focus on #04, November 2010.

10. Anes Alic and Vildana Skocajic, "Understanding Bosnia, Part One," *ISN Security Watch*, February 26, 2009.

11. "Public Opinion Poll, Bosnia and Herzegovina, BiH, August 2010," Washington, DC: National Democratic Institute, p. 5.

12. "Independent Evaluation of the National Youth Policy in Bosnia-Herzegovina," UN, Sarajevo, April 29, 2005.

13. Index Mundi puts Bosnia's estimated 2012 total fertility rate at 1.24 children born to each woman of childbearing age; a rate of 2.1 is required to maintain a population. See *www.indexmundi.com/bosnia_and_herzegovina/demographics_profile.html*.

14. See *The Failed States Index 2013*, available from *ffp.statesindex.org/rankings-2013-sortable*.

15. "NATO's Relations with Bosnia and Herzegovina," NATO website, available from *www.nato.int/cps/en/natolive/topics_49127.htm*.

16. Steven Woehrel, "Bosnia and Herzegovina: Current Issues and U.S. Policy," *Congressional Research Service, (CRS) Report R40479,* Washington, DC: CRS, January 24, 2013.

17. "Bosnia and Herzegovina 2012 Progress Report," European Commission SWD (2012) 335 Final, Brussels, Belgium, October 10, 2012, pp. 4-5.

18. "Bosnia's Human Rights Record Hinders EU talks." *EurAktiv.com*, May 24, 2013.

19. See, for example, the European Commission's belabored analysis: "[a] shared vision among the political representatives on the overall direction and future of the country and its institutional set-up for the qualitative step forward on the country's EU path remain absent." Quoted in "Commission Proposes Candidate Statue for Albania," *EurAktiv.com*, October 11, 2012.

20. Christopher Deliso, *The Coming Balkan Caliphate: The Threat of Radical Islam to Europe and the West,* Westport, CT: Praeger Security International, 2007, p. 8.

21. Evan Kohlmann, *Al-Qaida's Jihad in Europe: The Afghan-Bosnian Network*, Oxford, UK: Berg, 2004, pp. xii-xiii.

22. John R. Schindler, *Unholy Terror: Bosnia, Al-Qa'ida, and the Rise of Global Jihad*, St. Paul, MN: Zenith Press, 2007, pp. 295-309.

23. Kohlmann, *Al-Qaida's Jihad in Europe*, pp. 224-225.

24. Suzana Mijatovic, "Tajna Diplomatska Ofanziva Iranaca u BiH," *Slobodna Bosna*, October 25, 2012.

25. Christopher Deliso, "Israeli Security Concerns and the Balkans," *Balkananalysis.com*, March 31, 2013, p. 14.

26. Woehrel, "Bosnia and Herzegovina."

27. "Country Reports on Terrorism," Washington, DC: US Department of State, May 20, 2013; and "EU Terrorism Situation and Trend Report, Te-Sat," European Police Agency, 2013.

28. Quoted in Vlado Azinović, Kurt Bassuener, and Bodo Weber, "Assessing the Potential for Renewed Ethnic Violence in Bosnia and Herzegovina: A Security Risk Analysis," Berlin, Germany: Atlantic Initiative and Democratization Policy Council, October 2011, p. 69.

29. Azinović, Bassuener, and Weber, "A Security Risk Analysis," pp. 65-66.

30. Quoted in Vildana Skocajic and Anes Alic, "Understanding Bosnia, Part Four," *ISN Security Watch*, March 12, 2009.

31. Anes Alic, "Wahhabism: from Vienna to Bosnia," *ISN*, April 6, 2007.

32. Robert Coalson and Maja Nikolic, "Radical Islamists Seek to Exploit Frustration in Bosnia," *RFE/RL*, March 1, 2013.

33. Walter Mayr, "Islamists Gain Ground in Sarajevo," *Islamist Watch*, February 25, 2009.

34. Skocajic and Alic, "Understanding Bosnia, Part Four."

35. *Ibid*.

36. Sylvia Poggioli, "Radical Islam Uses Balkan Poor To Wield Influence," *NPR*, October 25, 2010.

37. See Steven Oluic, "Radical Islam on Europe's Frontier—Bosnia & Herzegovina," *National Security and the Future*, Vol. 1-2, No. 9, 2008, p. 42; and Ioannis Michaletos, "An Outlook of Radical Islamism in Bosnia." *Pakistan Christian Post*, July 2, 2012.

38. "Saudis Tied to Domineering Wahabi Presence in Bosnia," *WorldTribune.com*, March 27, 2007.

39. Nenad Pejic, "Wahhabist Militancy in Bosnia Profits from Local and International Inaction," The Jamestown Foundation, *Terrorism Monitor*, Vol. 9, Issue 42, November 17, 2011.

40. Schwartz, "Bosnia Re-arrests Top Wahhabi Plotter."

41. Juan Carlos Antunez Moreno, *Foreign Influences in Islam in Bosnia and Herzegovina since 1995*, The Islam in South East Europe Forum (ISEEF), Sarajevo, Bosnia, 2010.

42. "Vast Majority of Bosnian Federation TV Viewers See Wahhabism as a Threat," *BBC*, December 10, 2006.

43. Quoted in Stephen Schwartz, "Bosnia Cracks Down on Wahhabism," *The Weekly Standard*, February 18, 2010.

44. Quoted in Boris Kanzleiter, "Wahhabi Rules: Extremism Comes to Bosnia," *World Politics Review*, May 2, 2007.

45. See official Izetbegović biography, available from *www.predsjednistvobih.ba/biogr/?cid=8148,1,1*.

46. Deliso, *The Coming Balkan Caliphate*, p. 7.

47. Soldo, "Muslim Politician Says Bosnian Al-Qa'idah Can 'Destabilize Europe'," *Vecernij list*, December 11, 2007, translated by *BBC Monitoring International Reports*, December 14, 2007.

48. S. Dusanic, "Bakir Izetbegovic Gave Land to Saudi Committee as Present," *Glas Srpske*, May 29, 2008, translated by *BBC Montoring Europe, Political*, May 29, 2008.

49. Walter Mayr, "The Prophet's Fifth Column: Islamists Gain Ground in Sarajevo," *Der Spiegel*, February 25, 2009.

50. Berina Mulabegovic, "Who is Bakir Izetbegovic?" *Globalia Magazine*, May 12, 2010.

51. "Bosna Bank International Holds Annual Board Meeting in Dubai," available from *www.ameinfo.com*, December 19, 2012. BBI shareholders include the Islamic Development Bank, the Dubai Islamic Bank, and the Abu Dhabi Islamic Bank.

52. Timur Kuran, *Islam and Mammon: The Economic Predicaments of Islamism*, Princeton, NJ: Princeton University Press, 2004, p. 6.

53. The two signed several memoranda of understanding on economic cooperation in 2010. The following year saw strengthened scientific and research ties between Iran and Bosnian universities, while in 2012, they pledged to expand economic ties. See "Iran, Bosnia Sign MoUs on Economic Cooperation," *Fars News Agency*, May 1, 2010; "Iran, Bosnia Universities to Strength-

en Scientific, Research Ties," *IRNA*, December 3, 2011; and "Iran, Bosnia Urge Enhancement of Bilateral Relations," *PressTV*, April 10, 2012.

54. "Izetbegovic Meets Ahmadinejad in Cairo," *BiH Dayton Project*, February 8, 2013, available from *www.bihdaytonproject. com/?p=1793*.

55. Mijatovic, "Tajna Diplomska Ofanziva Iranaca u BiH," *Slobodna Bosna*, October 25, 2012.

56. Radončić was originally close to Alija Izetbegović. He has used nationalist rhetoric and donations to the Islamic Community to advance his political career. See "Bosnia—Good Bosniaks, Bad Bosniaks, Good Muslims, Bad Muslims," State Department cable Sarajevo 103, January 27, 2009, provided courtesy of Wikileaks.

57. The report of Izetbegovic's involvement appeared in an investigation by the Bosnian Serb newspaper, *Glas Srbske*, according to Benjamin Weinthal, "Bosnia Tells Iranian Spies to Leave to No Avail," *The Jerusalem Post*, May 9, 2013. Also see Benjamin Weinthal, "Bosnia Expels Two Iranian Diplomats," *The Jerusalem Post*, April 28, 2013; and Weinthal, "Bosnia Expels Alleged Iranian Spies," *The Jerusalem Post*, May 19, 2013.

58. "Bosnia Expels Third Iranian Diplomat," *Iran Daily Brief*, June 28, 2013, available from *www.irandailybrief.com/2013/06/28/ bosnia-expels-third-iranian-diplomat/*.

59. Mijatovic, "Tajna Diplomska Ofanziva Iranaca u BiH."

60. Oluic, "Radical Islam on Europe's Frontier," p. 46.

61. Schindler, *Unholy Terror*, p. 200.

62. "Haris Silajdzic: The Unexposed Zealot," Toronto, Ontario, Canada: The Centre for Peace in the Balkans, October 2002.

63. Oluic, "Radical Islam on Europe's Frontier," p. 47.

64. Soldo, "Muslim Politician Says Bosnian Al-Qa'idah Can 'Destabilize Europe'," *Vecernij list*, December 11, 2007, translated by *BBC Monitoring International Reports*, December 14, 2007.

65. For example, Cornell University stated that "Silajdzic today represents the forces for an integrated, secular and multinational Bosnia. He continues to demand the right of return of refugees and displaced persons and is a proponent of multiethnicity, political pluralism and parliamentary democracy in the country." See *news.cornell.edu/stories/1997/09/co-prime-minister-bosnia-and-herzegovina-will-visit-cornell-and-deliver-bartels*.

66. "Obituary: Alija Izetbegovic," *BBC News*, October 19, 2003.

67. Alija Izetbegović, *The Islamic Declaration: A Programme for the Islamization of Muslims and the Muslim People*, Sarajevo, Bosnia, 1990.

68. "Verdict of the Federal Court," Kps — 108/84, available from *www.slobodanpraljak.com/MATERIJALI/RATNI%20DOKUMENTI/islamska%20deklaracija/VERDICT_OF_THE_FEDERAL_COURT.pdf*.

69. The *Declaration* was actually reissued not by Izetbegović, but by a Serbian company owned by notorious Bosnian Serb leader, Vojislav Seselj. See Schindler, *Unholy Terror*, p. 63.

70. Schindler, *Unholy Terror*, p. 200.

71. See "Karadzic Talks Izetbegovic in Cross-Examination," *Balkaninsight.com*, April 26, 2010; and Rachel Erwin, "Bosnian Serb Leader Says Karadzic Was Peacemaker," Washington, DC: Institute for War and Peace Reporting, April 12, 2013.

72. See Schindler, *Unholy Terror*, pp. 32-45. The actual indictment does not name Iran. See "Verdict of the Federal Court."

73. Schindler, *Unholy Terror*, p. 54. See also "Bosnian Threatens Poison Gas Against Serb Forces," *The New York Times*, October 31, 1992.

74. *Ibid*. p. 52.

75. See the obituary by Enes Karic, "Alija Izetbegovic, President of Bosnia," Sarajevo, Bosnia, available from *www.muslim-lawyers.net/news/index.php3?aktion=show&number=243*.

76. "Alija Izetbegovic: His Background and Philosophies," London, UK: Balkan Research Centre, December 1992.

77. J. Millard Burr and Robert O. Collins, *Alms for Jihad: Charity and Terrorism in the Islamic World*, Cambridge, MA: Cambridge University Press, 2006, pp. 140-143.

78. Schindler, *Unholy Terror*, p. 52.

79. In this first trial, Izetbegović was convicted of terrorist activities related to the Young Muslims.

80. Schindler, *Unholy Terror*, pp. 107-108.

81. "Bosnia Fire Official with Ties to Iran," *Los Angeles Times*, November 20, 1996.

82. Nidzara Ahmetasevic, Adnan Butorovic, and Mirsad Fazlic, "Fishers of Children's Souls: Third Offensive of Young Muslims," *Slobodna Bosna*, January 30, 2003, English translation, May 10, 2004.

83. See testimony by Eve-Ann Prentice at the Milosević trial at the ICTY, available from *www.youtube.com/watch?v=IUDznadBOZU*.

84. Schindler, *Unholy Terror*, p. 254.

85. *Ibid.*, pp. 263-266. See also Azinović, Bassuener, and Weber, "A Security Risk Analysis," p. 65; and Ivo Lučić, "Bosnia and Herzegovina and Terrorism," *National Security and the Future*, Vol. 2, No. 3-4, Autumn/Winter 2001.

86. Azinović, Bassuener, and Weber, "A Security Risk Analysis," p. 65.

87. Quoted in Schindler, *Unholy Terror*, p. 263, sourced to an article in *Slobodna Bosna*, September 13, 2001. "Salam" is a greeting, while "tekbir" means the phrase "Allahu akbar."

88. Mike O'Connor, "Spies for Iranians Are Said to Gain a Hold in Bosnia," *The New York Times*, November 28, 1997.

89. He reportedly said that the Bosniak secret police "had been infected by al-Qa-ida . . . there was virtually a cell of that organization there." See quote in Schindler, *Unholy Terror*, p. 240.

90. Ena Latin, "Sarajevo Trial May Lift Lid on Assassinations," Washington, DC: Institute for War and Peace Reporting, May 22, 2002; and "Ex-Bosnian Officials Arrested for Terrorism and Espionage Walk Free," *AFP*, October 1, 2002.

91. See OHR decision, available from *www.ohr.int/decisions/removalssdec/default.asp?content_id=28446*. Ashdown fired him for failure to handle intelligence information properly.

92. Nenad Pejic, "Wahhabist Militancy in Bosnia Profits from Local and International Inaction," The Jamestown Foundation *Terrorism Monitor*, Vol. 9, Issue 42, November 17, 2011.

93. Quoted in Stefano Giantin, "A Bosnian Plea: 'Italians, Don't Give Peace Prize to Cerić," *eurasiareview.com*, February 27, 2012.

94. "Grand Mufti Ceric Awarded Italian Foundation Peace Prize," *The Global Muslim Brotherhood Daily Report*, March 26, 2012.

95. See text of "A Declaration of European Muslims," available from *www.rferl.org/content/article/1066751.html*.

96. "Bosnian Grand Mufti Says Islamic Law Compatible With Constitution, Will Visit Iran," *Global Muslim Brotherhood Daily Report*, June 8, 2009.

97. Kenneth Morrison, "Wahhabism in the Balkans," Balkan Series 08/06, Swindon, Wiltshire, UK: Defence Academy of the United Kingdom, Advanced Research and Assessment Group, February 2008, p. 9.

98. Patrick Moore, "Leader of Bosnia's Islamic Community Speaks Out," *RFE/RL*, April 23, 2004.

99. "Bosnia—Rising toward Trouble," Embassy Sarajevo, Bosnia, February 16, 2009, provided courtesy of Wikileaks.

100. See, for example, "The Second Report on Islamophobia, January—December 2011," Islamic Community of Bosnia and Herzegovina, Sarajevo, March 2012.

101. "Bosnians Elect New Grand Mufti; Mustafa Ceric Replaced After 19 Years," *The Global Muslim Brotherhood Daily Report*, September 25, 2012.

102. "Bosnia's Dangerous Tango: Islam and Nationalism," Brussels, Belgium: International Crisis Group, February 26, 2013, p. 1.

103. Quoted in Soldo, "Muslim Politician."

104. Ahmad ibn Naqib al-Misri, *Reliance of the Traveller: A Classic Manual of Islamic Sacred Law*, Beltsville, MD: Amana publications, 1994, o.25.3, p. 640. Exceptions to this rule occurred in Islamic empires, but the individuals who occupied such positions were always vulnerable to attack.

105. *Ibid.*, pp. 607-609.

106. Aleksa Djilas, "The Nation that Wasn't," Nader Mousavizadeh, ed., *The Black Book of Bosnia*, New York: HarperCollins Publishers 1996, p. 25.

107. Alija Izetbegović, *The Islamic Declaration: A Programme for the Islamization of Muslims and the Muslim Peoples*, Sarajevo, Bosnia, 1990.

108. Available from EUFOR website, *www.euforbih.org/*. In fact, Turkey has offered to make up shortfalls in EUFOR staffing but had been rebuffed by the EU, apparently for fear that EUFOR would effectively become a "TurkFor." See Azinović, Bassuener, and Weber, "A Security Risk Analysis," p. 72.

109. Anes Alic, "Turkey's Growing Influence in the Balkans," *oilprice.com*, June 9, 2010.

110. Dusan Stojanovic, "Turkey Uses Economic Clout to Gain Balkan Foothold," *The Seattle Times*, March 13, 2011.

111. This nostalgia, shared by the Muslim Brotherhood, found its way into Izetbegović's *Declaration*, in which he mourned the replacement of the Ottoman Empire by a secular Turkish regime whose new generation "had lost the remembrance of its past." See Izetbegović, *Islamic Declaration*, p. 14.

112. Esad Hećimović, "Šta Turska hoće na Balkanu?" *Dani*, October 23, 2009. See English translation of excerpts at *grayfalcon. blogspot.com.*

113. John Eibner, "Turkey's Christians Under Siege," *Middle East Quarterly*, Vol. 18, No. 2, Spring 2011.

114. "What Lies Beneath Ankara's New Foreign Policy," State Department cable Ankara 87, November 29, 2010, provided courtesy of Wikileaks.

115. Patrick Goodenough, "OIC Fulfills Function of Caliphate, Embodies 'Islamic Solidarity,' Says OIC Chief," *CNS News*, May 10, 2010.

116. Kenan Efendic, "OIC Invites Bosnia to Become Full Member," *Balkan Insight*, April 16, 2013.

117. Available from *www.oicun.org/articles/54/1/Cairo-Declaration-on-Human-Rights-in-Islam/1.html*.

118. "Turkey Trying to Keep Its Influence in Bosnia," State Department cable Ankara 1651, November 17, 2009, provided courtesy of Wikileaks.

119. Azinović, Bassuener, and Weber, "A Security Risk Analysis," pp. 31-34.

120. *Ibid.*, p. 33.

121. *Ibid.*, p. 34., italics in original.

122. See OSA website, available from *www.osa-oba.gov.ba/ osaobaeng.htm*.

123. Azinović, Bassuener, and Weber, "A Security Risk Analysis," p. 44.

124. *Ibid.*, pp. 39-52.

125. Mark Lowen, "Major Criminal Flees Bosnia Jail," *BBC*, July 29, 2009. Abu Hamza, a former member of Egyptian Gama'a al-Islamiyya, first arrived in Bosnia in 1992. See Anes Alic, "The Ringleaders of the Bosnia-Herzegovina Wahhabi Movement," The Jamestown Foundation *Terrorism Focus*, Vol. 4, Issue 6, March 23, 2007.

126. Azinović, Basseuner, and Weber, "A Security Risk Analysis," pp. 4-8.

127. Ratka Babic, "Bosnia Serbs Will Call Referendum on NATO," *Balkan Insight*, February 12, 2013.

128. Stefan J. Bos, "Report: 'Christians Flee Bosnia Amid Discrimination, Islamization," *BosNewsLife*, October 12, 2012.

129. "Bosnia and Herzegovina 2012 Progress Report," p. 17.

130. Janusz Bugajski, *Return of the Balkans: Challenges to European Integration and U.S. Disengagement*, Carlisle, PA: Strategic Studies Institute, U.S. Army War College, May 2013, pp. 156-158.

131. EUFOR Fact Sheet, available from *www.euforbih.org/index. php?option=com_content&view=article&id=15&Itemid=134*.

132. Azinović, Bassuener, and Weber, "A Security Risk Analysis," p. 72.

133. See European Union External Action website, available from *www.eeas.europa.eu/csdp/structures-instruments-agencies/*.

134. Azinović, Bassuener, and Weber, "A Security Risk Analysis," p. 72.

135. *Ibid.*

136. The top three missions are: assisting Bosnian authorities with reforms and commitments related to the Partnership for Peace and closer integration with NATO; providing logistic and other support to EUFOR; and supporting ICTY on a case-by-case basis. See "NATO's Relations with Bosnia and Herzegovina," available from *www.nato.int*.

137. Charles G. Boyd, "Making Peace with the Guilty: The Truth about Bosnia," *Foreign Affairs*, Vol. 74, No. 50, September/ October 1995, pp. 22-38.

138. Edward P. Joseph, "Bosnia-Herzegovina," *The Western Balkans Policy Review 2010*, Washington, DC: Center for Strategic and International Studies, pp. 63-64.

139. Oluic, "Radical Islam on Europe's Frontier," p. 48.